God Even Likes My Pantry

Meditations for Munchers

MAB GRAFF HOOVER

Daybreak Books

Zondervan Publishing House
Grand Rapids, Michigan

GOD EVEN LIKES MY PANTRY
Copyright © 1983 by The Zondervan Corporation
Grand Rapids, Michigan

Daybreak Books are published by Zondervan
Publishing House, 1415 Lake Drive, S.E.,
Grand Rapids, Michigan 49506

Library of Congress Cataloging in Publication Data

Hoover, Mab Graff.
    God even likes my pantry.
    1. Dieters—Prayer-books and devotions—English.   I. Title.
BV4596.D53H66   1983   242'.86   83-14565
ISBN 0-310-47012-9

All scripture quotations, unless otherwise noted, are taken from the
HOLY BIBLE: NEW INTERNATIONAL VERSION (North American
Edition). Copyright © 1978 by The International Bible Society. Used
by permission of Zondervan Bible Publishers.

Edited by Evelyn Bence
Illustrated by Martha Bentley

Printed in the United States of America

87   88   89   90   91 / 9   8   7   6   5

Contents

Introduction

Why had I bought a book titled *Free to Be Thin?* I sighed as I turned it over and read the red-letter blurb: "How to Lose Weight FOREVER!" Dieting! I hated the subject. What had possessed me to buy it?

True, I needed to lose weight, but I already owned half a dozen diet books. They all said the same thing—starve and lose, eat and gain. How well I knew. While I've never been mistaken for the fat lady in a circus, I'd always been overweight. Crash dieting, with the inevitable regaining, had been a way of life for me since high school, where I learned fellows don't favor fat.

"But I'm not a teenager anymore," I grumbled. "Don't I deserve to relax? So I don't look like a model—who cares?"

I cared!

I turned and looked at myself in the full-length mirror. I hated my fat stomach and the lumps on my hips. Yet every year it got harder to face another diet.

My husband was no help. He enjoyed eating and didn't want me to diet. "If you keep going on those fad diets you'll ruin your health," he scolded. "I'll tell you when I think you're fat." Of course, that kind of talk always lulled me for a while—long enough to gobble more Danish pastry, candy bars, and hot fudge sundaes.

I walked away from the mirror and sadly shook my head. I not only hated how . . . lumpy I looked, I was worried. Maybe ten pounds overweight wasn't bad, but I was on an upward streak, out of control. After a long, fat summer I was trying to work up the courage to start another diet. That's why I bought the book by Marie Chapian. I picked it up again. "How to Lose Weight FOREVER," it shouted. "I'll bet!" I shouted back. Half-heartedly, I began to read.

It took a couple of days but I read it all the way through and was impressed with the author's knowledge of nutrition. She had learned what foods are necessary to good health and what foods are harmful. I almost quit reading, though, when I learned she counted calories. "Just another dumb diet book," I growled. I was intrigued, however, when I read, "Ask yourself this question: Will I allow the Holy Spirit to take over my eating habits?"[1] And my eyes really popped when I read, "Ask the Lord how much *He* wants you to weigh."[2] Readers who sincerely wanted to lose weight were instructed to get a notebook, a Bible, and a calorie counter and to have a time of communication with the Lord every morning, before breakfast. They were encouraged to put themselves into God's hands—to ask Him to make it clear how much they were to weigh and how many calories a day He wanted them to eat! I'd been a Christian for many years and had prayed about everything

---

[1]Marie Chapian, *Free to Be Thin* (Minneapolis, Minn.: Bethany Fellowship, Inc., 1979). p. 15.
[2]Ibid., p. 25.

—especially for will power when I began a diet—but I'd never asked the Lord how much He wanted me to weigh or how many calories a day I should eat. It almost seemed sacrilegious to ask God such *fleshly* things! Yet Proverbs 3:5–6 says:

Trust in the LORD with all your heart and lean not on your own understanding; in all your ways acknowledge him, and he will make your paths straight.

Did that include my weight? Did that include what I was to eat?

With a tiny hope stirring inside, I bought a notebook (I already had a calorie counter), and, the next morning, with Bible, book, and counter, I had my first meeting with the Lord to get "intake instructions." I was on the program!

How exciting to see that old scale needle start down —but even more exciting was my discovery of how many Bible verses can be used to teach and encourage good eating habits. What a thrill to learn that our Lord Jesus is interested not only in our spiritual beauty, but our physical beauty.

Are you like I was—tired of being overweight, yet dreading the start of another diet? Why don't you try asking Him how much He wants you to weigh (it might be more than you think!) and how much you're supposed to eat each day? Then trust Him to give you the strength to stay with it. He gave me that power, and I know He'll give it to you, too. God does expect us to use our brains though, so we need to find out what foods are good for us and how much we should eat. If you don't know much about nutrition or how to count calories, you might want to read one or more of the many excellent books available on nutrition, such as *Let's Try Real Food,* by Ethel Renwick (Zondervan) and *Let's Stay Healthy: A Guide to Lifelong Nutrition* by Adelle Davis (Harcourt Brace Jovanovich Inc.)

God Even Likes My Pantry isn't another diet book. There aren't any menus or nutritional nuggets in it. It is a collection of "diet devotions"—thoughts and prayers, written in my little notebook as I met with the Lord each morning to receive His instructions and strength that enabled me to stay on a healthful food program. If you read one or two a day they may help you think about the Lord instead of food. Through Christ I have reached my goal! My thought life in regard to food has been revolutionized. I no longer want rich, sweet, fat foods in my body. But because I know I could slide back into the old eating habits, I don't trust myself. Every day I intend to seek His guidance about food—for the rest of my life.

I want Him always to like my pantry.

Beginning—Again

Here I go again. I've tried to diet so many times I've lost count. How many times have I promised myself, *This time I'll succeed?* I'm not sure I can bear another failure. But I'm going to try this "Bible method"—maybe it is the answer.

> *We pray . . . you may live a life worthy of the Lord and may please him in every way: . . . being strengthened with all power according to his glorious might so that you may have great endurance and patience (Col. 1:10–11).*

Does being fat or slender have anything to do with living a life worthy of the Lord? Sure, I *know* I am supposed to please God and bring honor to His name. But doesn't that mean spiritually? Or does it include my figure? I know my body is the temple of God—so (sigh, groan) of course it means my figure.

But I hate to diet. I hate to exercise. I love to eat.

And yet, that verse says I can be *strengthened* with *all* power, according to God's glorious might. Think of that. His power and might made the whole universe—that's a lot of power. Is that mighty power really available to unlovable, fat me? The Bible says I can have it all. I believe the Bible is true, so surely, I will have endurance and patience to stay with this food plan—at least for today.

Lord Jesus, You have always been the power available to me—I just fail to use it. Don't let me fail this time.

Two Heads Are *Not* Better

Two minor miracles to report! Even though I kept my calorie count to a mere 1050, I wasn't hungry in the night as I usually am when dieting. I slept well. *And*—oh joy—I have already lost a pound. I couldn't believe it this morning when I gently stepped onto the scale, so I jumped on it! When it quieted down, its verdict stood true!

For by him [Jesus] all things were created: . . . by him and for him. . . . He is the head of the body . . . so that in everything he might have the supremacy (Col. 1:16–18).

Jesus created me. I was born a normal baby. He intended for me to grow up normally. I'm sure He didn't want me to be overweight. What is really amazing is that He created me for Himself. Why? Why did He bother? So that in everything—even in me—He might have the supremacy. He is the Head of my body. There can't be two heads. Or can there? Am I going to argue with Him? Or worse, ignore Him? When His still, small voice whispers, "Don't eat that," am I going to obey?

Lord, I bow to Your authority to rule in my body today—but don't forget how hungry and cross I get around four o'clock. So please overrule any sneaky or willful thought I might have to go off the food program.

Going Down

I've lost some weight! I can't tell if it's half a pound or three-quarters of a pound, but the needle on the scale is moving in the right direction! Hurray! I'm so excited that I'm tempted to skip breakfast and lose even faster. But that's not part of the program. I am learning to eat right—no more stuffing then starving for me.

I [Paul] ... delight to see how orderly you are and how firm your faith in Christ is. So then, just as you received Christ Jesus as Lord, continue to live in him, rooted and built up in him, strengthened in the faith ... and overflowing with thankfulness (Col. 2:5-7).

It is so hard for me to be orderly, to do things in their proper sequence, to be disciplined—especially when it comes to food. In the past, after gorging, I would cry out, "God! Work a miracle. Make me feel good, and remove this fat!" But God is a God of order. The only way this fat is going to come off is by my eating right, day in and day out. That takes faith. Do I have faith? When I received Christ as Savior, I simply accepted what He had already done on the cross for me. That was faith. This verse tells me that just as I received Christ as Lord, I am to continue to live in Him. How can I do this in regard to losing weight? Before I eat something wrong, I must stop and take time to call out to Him for help. Every time I do this, my faith will get stronger—and so will my will power.

Dear Lord, thank You that my weight is going down. I am sincerely overflowing with thankfulness this morning. By faith I reach out and receive enough strength from You to eat only what You want me to.

It's Good for You!

Today, before I went to lunch with Sue, I was afraid my determination to eat right might fail. She and I have always binged together. But before I left the house I prayed that no matter what scrumptious pictures appeared on the menu or how delicious a meal was described, I would order two poached eggs and whole wheat toast, period. The Lord strengthened my backbone. I even resisted Sue's attempts to get me to match her order of pancakes and an omelet. "Cheese and ham are good for you!" she insisted. But I looked up at the waitress and said, "Two poached eggs, please, and an order of whole wheat toast." I felt terrific—even when Sue poured on the boysenberry syrup!

See to it that no one takes you captive through hollow and deceptive philosophy, which depends on human tradition and the basic principles of this world rather than on Christ (Col. 2:8).

All during lunch we talked about different diets and I think my attitudes have matured. This time I am not trying to lose weight fast—just so I can turn around and binge again. I am determined to eat properly—to take care of this wonderful body Jesus created. I *must not* be influenced by anyone to eat junk foods or fats or sugars, just because "We've always eaten this way."

O Lord Jesus, help me see through the traditional arguments for why I should eat the old way, and help me be content with the new way. I'm depending on You.

DID YOU HAFTA SAY, "TEN TEASPOONS OF SUGAR IN A SINGLE SLICE OF FRUIT PIE?

I Can't Believe I Ate and Ate

There aren't words to describe my self-hate and frustration this morning. I *gained* a pound! Why did I fail last night? I had been so good at lunch. Maybe that was the reason. Maybe my guard was down because I was feeling a little cocky about the victory. I don't know. All I know is I really stuffed myself—peanuts, cheese, toast—all good food—I just didn't count the calories.

Since . . . you [Mab] *have been raised with Christ, set your heart on things above, where Christ is seated at the right hand of God. Set your mind on things above, not on earthly things* [like what's in the refrigerator] *(Col. 3:1–2).*

I *know* I have been raised with Christ, so even though I blew it last night, I *will set* my mind today—with God's help! At the beginning of this program He told me to stay on 1050 calories a day. I must have eaten 3050 yesterday.

Forgive me, Lord, for disobeying You by eating more than You want me to. And help me not to become overly confident after I've had a good day, because overconfidence leads to failure.

YOU'RE KIDDING ME!
FOUR TEASPOONS OF SUGAR IN ONE SERVING OF CANNED FRUIT? I THOUGHT FRUIT WAS DIET FOOD.

Big Fat Lies

What a relief! I've lost that pound I gained when I "pigged out" the other night. If I never believed it before, I now know that Jeremiah 17:9 is true: "The heart is deceitful above all things." I told myself that peanuts were too small to contain many calories and that cheese was good for me. I even ate yogurt with syrupy fruit at the bottom, telling myself that if I didn't eat a little something sweet I'd get discouraged and quit dieting altogether. Lies—all lies. Jeremiah goes on to say that the heart is beyond cure. So what am I to do? The only way I can control my body is to study the Bible, claim the promise of a verse, and pray.

> For you [Mab] died, and your life is now hidden with Christ in God. . . . Put to death, therefore, whatever belongs to your earthly nature: sexual immorality, impurity, lust, evil desires and greed, which is idolatry. (Col. 3:3–5).

19

I try to imagine what it is like to be dead. When mother died, the body looked like my mother, but it wasn't she. Mother liked to eat, but that body never grew hungry. Even though her body had no appetite, I knew mother was still alive—hidden from me, but alive in Christ. The apostle Paul says that *my* life also is hidden with Christ; because I have died to self, I am commanded to kill my earthly nature!

No more pretending; lust for food is unmasked. It is idolatry! And all these years I thought I worshiped only Christ. . .

Oh help me, Lord Jesus, to put to death this lust for food. Take over in my body this whole day and evening.

Sticks and Stones

Although the weight hasn't plummeted, I'm encouraged with its steady decline. I'm even able to zip up a pair of pants I *used* to wear! I've actually been feeling rather slender, beautiful, and happy, until yesterday at church.

After the service, while we were standing around talking, I confided to one of my friends that I had been on the food program for several weeks. She looked me up and down; a surprised and puzzled expression crossed her face; her gaze returned to my stomach, and she said, "Really?" "You don't look any different."

GR-R-R-rr! I felt like exploding right there in the foyer. I wanted to tell her I didn't think she looked like Cheryl Tiegs either. I wanted to rush to "hot fudge haven," but the weeks of discipline, plus the power of Jesus, enabled me to smile and shrug it off, thinking she probably needed a new pair of glasses.

Praise God! for Jesus said:

Blessed are those who hunger and thirst for [hot dogs? hot fudge sundaes? No!] *righteousness, for they will be filled (Matt. 5:6).*

If I am to reach my weight-goal I cannot dwell on what others say or what I think I want or even on this food program. My mind must be steadily locked in on the Lord.

O Jesus, help me to be hungry and thirsty, not for food or drink, but for righteousness.
(Righteousness is the opposite of wrongness.)

Food for Thought

If anyone reads this diary after I'm dead and gone, I hope they won't think that all I ever thought about was food. There are so many other things I'm interested in: I love to garden, and I enjoy my church activities, especially singing in the choir; I spend some time oil painting (I'm not very good, but it's fun); I'm interested in everything my *unusually bright* children do. But jotting down my thoughts, victories, failures, and prayers about food really helps me stay on the program. Maybe the actual writing is like a therapy, or maybe the extra study in the Word encourages me, or maybe my late afternoon rereading of the diary, refreshes me and reminds me of how I felt in the morning, I don't know exactly how, but something (Someone) is working! Thank You, Lord.

And whatever you do, whether in word or deed, do it all in the name of the Lord Jesus, giving thanks to God the Father through him (Col. 3:17).

I paraphrased this verse and stuck it on the refrigerator: And whatever you eat, eat it in the name of the Lord Jesus.

Can I imagine myself picking up a grease-filled, chocolate-covered donut, and saying, "I eat this in the name of the Lord Jesus"? (!) Certain verses are so well known they seem to lose their power. But like TNT they are powerless only when not being used.

Dear Father, help me to take the time to think about everything I eat and be sure I can honestly eat it in Your name.

Monkey See, Monkey Do

We're going over to Mom Hoover's today after church. In honor of Pat's birthday all the family will be there. It will be the first time I've been with the whole family since I started on the program, and I'm scared. We all bring food—fancy salads and desserts. And mom always has a spread of fried chicken, mashed potatoes and gravy, and homemade bread. How can I resist all that temptation!

You became imitators of us [Paul] *and of the Lord; in spite of severe suffering . . . you became a model to all the believers (1 Thess. 1:6–7).*

I can't imagine Paul with an ounce of excess fat, surely he was too interested in being a witness for Jesus Christ to think about all the goodies he could eat. And, surely, the Lord's body was perfect. Therefore, if I am going to imitate Paul and Jesus, I must eat as they must have—*sparingly!* I do want to be a model to other believers, or, more accurately, I don't want to be a stumbling block to anyone by being an overweight Christian. Today, I will eat one piece of chicken (without the skin), a lot of salad (chewing it well), some vegetables, fruit, and one small slice of bread! I will imitate the Lord.

Lord Jesus, today as I sit at mom's table, help me be like You. Help me to be more interested in each member of the family than in each dish of food.

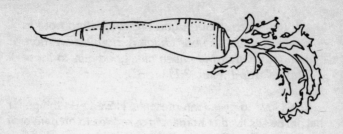

Carrots—Delicious!

Yesterday Joanie, a teacher, had the afternoon off and called to see if I had time to meet her in the shopping mall. Did I have time—for my darling daughter? I'm ashamed to admit it, but I was so anxious to meet her I broke the speed limit a couple of times. She looked wonderful to me, and just being with her for a little while swelled my heart with love and joy.

"Mother," she said, raising an eyebrow. "I'm on a diet. Let's *not* get hot fudge sundaes."

"Did you forget that I'm on a food program too?"

"That's right! Good. We won't tempt each other."

If she had suggested hot fudge sundaes, would I have had one? I love to please Joan, and in the past that has sometimes meant eating (too much) together. But this time the money I would have spent on our lunch and dessert bought her a pair of earrings.

If you, then, though you are evil, know how to give good gifts to your children, how much more will your Father in heaven give good gifts to those who ask him! (Matt. 7:11).

Yes, I love to give Joan presents. I love to do things for her. If she still lived at home and asked me to prepare only diet foods for her, I *would.* If she asked me to help her stay on a diet, I would—in any way possible.

If I ask God to help me, will He do less? This verse says our Father in heaven will do *much more.*

Question: How can I get His help?

Answer: Those who *ask* get the good gifts.

I'm asking You, Father, to reprogram my brain! Make the foods that I used to think so wonderful—pecan pie, hot fudge sundaes, chocolate cake—unappetizing, and make me think of apples, oranges, and carrots as delightful delicacies.

Flesh or the Devil?

This morning I didn't put sugar on my cereal. I was surprised; it didn't taste bad (to think I've heaped on one or two spoonsful almost every morning of my life!) I'm learning to enjoy the taste of sugarless, low-salt foods. Most days I'm happy, but some days I'm rebellious—like when my friend Carol said she hoped I wouldn't become a fanatical purist! I started wondering if I was getting goofy over this stuff. Or when I struggle with a deep-down dissatisfaction. I don't exactly crave anything, yet I crave everything! Lord! Help!

But the Lord is faithful, and he will strengthen and protect you from the evil one (2 Thess. 3:3).

When I look at chocolates or a beautiful birthday cake or Danish pastries, it's hard for me to believe they are being offered through the Evil One. But I know from Scripture that Satan continually tries to ruin the temple of God, the church, (my body!). He is an angel of light—the designer of all temptations.

But this verse says the Lord is faithful and will strengthen me and protect me from Satan. Would God lie?

Dear God, through Your power I am still on the right calorie count. Thank You for that, but please take away this discontented feeling and protect me from You-know-who.

Thoughtful Thanksgiving

After church I sought out one of the older Christian women and asked her what she saw as the root problem behind discontentment. I wanted relief! (although I didn't actually admit to her my deep restlessness).

"Honey," she said, "I don't know about other folks, but I find I'm discontent when I quit being thankful."

Ouch!

But how can I feel thankful when I haven't lost an ounce in almost a week? I *know* I've been good, too, at least until last night when I ate a muffin, toast, peanuts, and a banana. (And that was after dinner.) After, all I'd been depriving myself of so much for so long that I deserved a break—and everything I ate *was* healthful.

Everything God created is good, and nothing is to be rejected if it is received with thanksgiving (1 Tim. 4:4).

See, I told myself, *it wasn't wrong to eat all those things.* But I couldn't get any further in my rationalizations. The second phrase of the verse stared me down. I wasn't thankful last night. I felt guilty; I wished I wouldn't eat anymore; then I wolfed down the rest. If I had taken time to thank the Lord sincerely for the muffin, and if I had dwelled on His goodness to me, He probably would have made me so content I wouldn't have eaten anything else. In fact, as I look back over the past few days, I see I haven't consciously thanked Him for all the tasty things I have swallowed. Of course we have said grace before each meal—but my thoughts have not matched my words. I've been feeling sorry for myself. I *have* quit being thankful.

Dear Jesus, forgive me for acting like a spoiled brat. Help me meditate on Your goodness; help me appreciate the wonderful things You provide for me; help me to receive my food with sincere thanksgiving.

Calorie Cheater Caught

I've been doing well the past week. I haven't felt hungry, and zipping up my slacks without them cutting me in two feels so good *and* I lost almost a pound. *However,* when I weighed this morning I discovered I had gained back half a pound! It was no mistake. I even took off my nightie and all my jewelry and tried it again. *What happened?*

How do I know? I have certainly taken the time to be thankful for each meal, and I have counted calories religiously. . . . Well, almost religiously. Maybe I've cheated . . . here and there. I must face it seriously. I have cheated. This program allows for no maybes. I have taken bigger helpings, I have quit measuring and weighing foods, I have guess-timated calories instead of looking them up. I must have thought that if I was sincerely thankful, those extra calories would't count. I just can't do it. I can't keep to 1050 calories!

A man with leprosy came to Him [Jesus] *and begged him on his knees, "If you are willing, you can make me clean." Filled with compassion, Jesus reached out his hand and touched the man. "I am willing," he said. "Be clean!" Immediately the leprosy left him and he was cured (Mark 1:40–42).*

That leper couldn't control his leprosy. No matter how much he prayed or what he rubbed on his skin or what he ate, nothing he could do would help. Do I think I control my weight? *I* prepare the food; *I* study the Bible; *I* pray; *I* give thanks. Do I really have control over my body? No, *I* don't have control. Only as I give God control, am I controlled. When I come to Jesus, as the leper came, and get on my knees, as he did, then Jesus can make me clean—and lean! In 1 Corinthians 9:27, Paul said he makes his body his slave. I want my body to be *my* slave, yet I know the control is in Christ.

Lord Jesus, it's hard for me to strike the balance between being self-controlled and completely yielded to Your control. Help me understand how to do it.

Tower Power

Things look different this morning. I know very well that when I listen to and obey my Savior, I have control. It really is so simple: First, I read His directives (the Bible). Then I ask Him for help to perform His desires. Then I tell my body to obey His instructions. My body is reasonably easy to control—if my mind is truly set on doing His will. "He is the head of the body," I read in Colossians, but my mind argues: "God won't care if I eat just one cookie—just one." No wonder my body seems uncontrollable; I am so double-minded!

I keep asking that the God of our Lord Jesus Christ . . . may give you . . . wisdom . . . I pray also that the eyes of your heart may be enlightened in order that you may know . . . his incomparably great power for us who believe. That power . . . which he exerted in Christ when he raised him from the dead and seated him at his right hand in the heavenly realms, far above all rule and authority (Eph. 1:17–21).

The power that raised Jesus from the dead *is mine today.* Can I believe that? He endured hours of torture before death took Him. He was in the tomb seventy-two hours before God's power brought Him back to life, then later lifted Him bodily to heaven, where He is now seated at God's right hand. Again, I ask myself, can I believe that same power is in me? Yes! I do believe I have that power in my body and in my mind. It is for me to use as surely as I use my mouth to speak, my hands to work, and my legs to run.

Thank You, dear Jesus, for this wisdom, and for letting me know for certain this incomparable power is in me. Help me use it today to see myself seated with You in the heavenlies, instead of grubbing around down here, looking for food.

WOE, IS ME!
HOW CAN I RESIST
SUCH A TEMPTING
BANANA SPLIT?
WHAT'S THAT? TWENTY-
FIVE TEASPOONS
OF SUGAR.?
I'LL *FIND*
A WAY TO
RESIST IT!

Indulge? Bulge

When I was thirty, mother made me a beautiful, black dress in a classic pattern that will never go out of style. Yet, I haven't been able to wear it for . . . too long. Yesterday I took it out of the garment bag. Although I couldn't zip it all the way up, I could, at least, get into it. What a thrill! I still have a long way to go, but we're going to make it—the Lord and I.

No longer live as the Gentiles do, in the futility of their thinking. They are darkened in their under-standing and separated from the life of God because of their ignorance that is in them due to the hardening of their hearts. . . . They have given themselves over to sensuality so as to indulge in every kind of impurity, with a continual lust for more (Eph. 4:17–19).

Fat people are everywhere! And everywhere people seem to eat—eat—eat. And it isn't just the "Gentiles,"

37

either, most of us Christians are too heavy. We can blame some of it on "fellowship," because it's more enticing to get together over *food.* Part of it can be blamed on brilliant TV, magazine, and billboard advertising which assaults our senses. But most overeating is because we *give* ourselves over to sensuality, so we can indulge! The more we indulge, the more we want. "Munchies" are like money— there's never enough.

Lord, today help me remember that thinking about wrong foods is futile—useless—worthless. Not only futile, but it leads to overindulgence which does not satisfy. You have opened my eyes, Lord Jesus. I am not ignorant of Your power to help when I'm hungry. It's up to me not to harden my heart.

Fad Diet—Bad Diet

One of my church friends is going on a fad diet. I tried to talk her out of it and told her about the food program. She shook her head emphatically. "Too slow. I've got to get this off fast." I told her I used to feel the same way, and, although the weight does come off fast on a crash diet, it won't stay off. I could tell she wasn't really listening, and long ago I learned you can't *make* someone change. I only hope I'll never revert to those old ways. I want to eat sensibly the rest of my life.

Be imitators of God . . . as dearly loved children and live a life of love, just as Christ loved us and gave himself up for us as a fragrant offering and sacrifice to God. But among you there must not be even a hint of sexual immorality, or of any kind of impurity, or of greed, because these are improper for God's holy people (Eph. 5:1–3).

Greed. What an awful word. In this verse it probably refers more to accumulating riches than to stuffing bodies, but I can remember when I used to gobble up one donut, lick my fingers, then wolf down another—and another! Greed. That word and immorality are in the same sentence. In God's eyes is greed as bad as adultery? What about the word *impurity?* Would some diet concoctions and artificial sweeteners fall into that category? One label warns that the contents have caused cancer in laboratory animals. Wouldn't I just about have to admit (grudgingly) that if it causes cancer it has to contain some kind of impurity? Foo! There are at least six cans of diet pop with artificial sweeteners in our refrigerator.

Greed. An excessive, extreme desire for something. Isn't my friend's fad diet, which stems from an extreme desire to be thin, a form of greed? And why do I allow myself to drink beverages that I know are impure? To satisfy a greedy desire for sweets!

Problems, Lord. Diet foods and diet sodas have helped me get through a lot of days. But if they are impure, they shouldn't be in my body. Won't You please help me to enjoy water? Help me imitate You. Help me be sensible, not greedy, in the way I diet.

Filled With the Spirit

A business acquaintance took my husband and me out to dinner last night at a plush restaurant. My filet mignon was delicious, the hot rolls heavenly, and the salad magnificent. I worried a little, since I couldn't figure out exactly how many calories I was eating. And yet, all during dinner, I experienced a sort of freedom, a knowledge that God was in control—especially when I had no problem turning down Black Forest cake!

Our host was a big man. When watching him eat, I saw why. He consumed three alcoholic drinks before dinner, a liter of wine with his prime rib platter, a side order of fried zucchini, a loaf of bread, and a huge piece of cake. All this was topped with a cherry cordial. He must have consumed two thousand calories in alcohol alone! He told me he needed a few drinks to unwind after a hard day. I told him I used to drink to relax, but had found true serenity when I asked Jesus Christ to take over my life. He smiled warmly and said, "I'll drink to that!"

41

Do not get drunk on wine, which leads to de-bauchery. Instead, be filled with the Spirit. (Eph. 5:18).

By God's grace I don't drink alcohol anymore, but I remember what it was like to toss down one drink after another, trying to relax, trying to feel good. Excessive indulgence in anything is debauchery (which means intemperance or seduction from morality). When I eat so fast I don't chew thoroughly and can barely get my breath, or when I eat so much I can scarcely move, I am guilty of excessive indulgence—debauchery.

Thank You, dear Holy Spirit, for controlling me last night so I didn't gain. I invite You to fill me again today. Fill me to the top so there won't be room for overeating.

One Eye Shut

It is Saturday morning. We have already had breakfast and I am just now taking time for devotions. With the family around, I struggle to stick to one piece of toast, fruit, and bran cereal as I watch everyone else gobble down bacon, eggs, and waffles.

Pray in the Spirit on all occasions with all kinds of prayers and requests. With this in mind, be alert. (Eph. 6:18).

Every weekend so far I've gained back some weight. When I wake up on Saturday morning and realize I don't have to hurry and that loved ones are home, I feel as if I'm on a mini-holiday. Somehow that fun-feeling brings on a binge.

It must stem from our pre-Christian days, when we used to drink more on the weekends. Have I simply replaced drinking with overeating? What a disgusting and fearful thought. Although I am making some headway (I no longer miss sweet foods through the week), on the weekends the lust for cakes, ice cream, donuts, and chocolate *anything* revives. If only my whole family would join me in changing their eating habits! I should take time to pray, but I feel irresponsible. *Mab, be alert!*

Lord Jesus, hold the line for me. I am weak, but You are strong.

Lost Weekend

Another *gained* weekend. I do not feel like reading the Bible. I do not feel like praying. I feel like crying. I didn't evey try to have devotions Sunday morning. We are always in such a rush to get ready for Sunday school and church that there's no time for private worship! Isn't that some commentary on a Christian life? I ate right for breakfast, however, at *my* suggestion, we went to a smorgasbord for lunch, and, after I completely blew it there, I decided I might as well eat junk the rest of the day—cake, ice cream, candy. The only good thing I can say is that I did not consume the quantities I once would have. But I paid for my carelessness; I not only gained, I was sick in the night.

No one can serve two masters. Either he will hate the one and love the other, or he will be devoted to the one and despise the other. You cannot serve both God and . . . [stomach?] *(Matt. 6:24).*

The problem with me and the weekends must be that I haven't really believed that it is God who wants me on 1050 calories a day, everyday—Saturday and Sunday included. I must not be truly convinced that it is God who does not want me to eat sickening sugary slop. But I was so sick in the night! Ugh. I think I am convinced.

Father, I humbly ask Your forgiveness for gluttony. I know it was You who whispered to my heart, 1050 calories every day.

Josephine and I

Ever since our cat Josephine was neutered she's been gaining weight. She is really a glutton, and I've had to put her on a diet. After she eats all her own food, I've caught her nudging our cat Samson away from his dish. I've started feeding them in separate places and removing any leftovers. But poor Josephine. All day she begs me for more food. She doesn't understand why I no longer feed her on demand. Because I feel sorry for her, I sometimes take her out in the back yard and point out butterflies, or play with a string—anything to get her mind off her hunger. But what distracts her best? Taking her in my lap, scratching her ears, and loving her. She gets soothed and usually falls asleep. What a lesson for me. Instead of "meowing" around the refrigerator with Josephine, I go outside and pull a few weeds or just look up, and my mind is pulled away from myself. What is sure to work? Going to the bedroom, getting on my knees before the Lord, and letting Him love me.

*Being confident of this, that he who began a good
work in you will carry it on to completion until the
day of Christ Jesus (Phil. 1:6).*

Getting my body in shape for God's glory *is* a good
work and I know He will complete it. He began that work
when He caused me to notice the book *Free to Be Thin.*
Of my own choice I would never have bought it, but *He
was beginning a good work in me!* Just as I love
Josephine and don't want her to be fat, God loves me and
doesn't want me to be fat!

*Dear Jesus, thank You for loving me enough to begin
a good work in me; I thank You even more for the
knowledge that You will complete it.*

Me, Myself, and I

This morning before he left for work, my husband held me tightly. "You feel pretty thin," he said.

What a beautiful sentence! My pride glowed.

"Oh Joe," I said modestly. "I've got pounds to get off before I reach my goal."

He looked right into my eyes. "I hope you'll still love me when you do."

My mouth opened. Was he worried?

"You character!" I hugged him. "Don't you know by now that next to God I love you the very most?"

After he left for work I looked at myself in the full-length mirror. I sucked in my stomach as far as it would go and held my breath.

Not bad, I thought. *Not bad at all.*

Do nothing out of selfish ambition or vain conceit, but in humility consider others better than your-selves. Each of you should look not only to your

49

own interests, but also to the interests of others (Phil. 2:3–4).

Do nothing out of selfish ambition or vain conceit!

What a knife-twisting verse. Everyday I run to God and cry for help to stay on the program, and claim it's for *His* glory. But what are my real motives? Self-glorification? Wasn't I thrilled when Joe said I was thin? I felt proud of the weight I'd lost and how much slimmer I looked in the mirror. *Watch out, Mab.* The Lord hates a proud and haughty look. My motives *have* to be pure.

Joe looked so serious this morning. Maybe he is feeling threatened. I told him I loved him the most, so instead of thinking about me, myself, and I today, I'm going to do something special for him. I may even polish his shoes.

Lord Jesus, I don't want to be proud or vain. Forgive me. Help me to think of others more than myself.

Caution: God Working

Polishing Joe's shoes paid off in four ways! First, after I took all his shoes outside, I decided to clean the closet. I couldn't bear to put those shiny shoes back down on a fuzz-covered floor. Then it didn't take long to put our clothes in order on the racks and throw out some things we haven't worn in years. Now the closet looks great! Second, I didn't think of eating *once* while I was doing the shoes or closet. That old cliche "An idle brain is the Devil's workshop" is still true. Third, Joe was so pleased about his shoes (also dumfounded) that he suggested I buy myself a new dress and pair of shoes. He said I had made him feel like a king. Fourth, the whole project made me happy.

For it is God who works in you to will and to act according to his good purpose (Phil. 2:13).

It *is* God working in me. I can feel it and see it. I wish I could hold onto this wonderful thought and the way I feel—forever. Just think, the great and only God, who willed the universe into being, is willing *me* to act according to His good (not evil) purpose. Why does He even bother with me, a person who has failed Him so many times? I feel like David when he cried, "What is man that you are mindful of him, the son of man that you are for him?" (Ps. 8:4).

Thank You, Lord God Almighty, for being in me, for working out Your will in my life, even though sometimes I'm not willing.

Suffering Is Sharing

It's cold and drizzly out this morning. I'm alone, the furnace is turned up, and I'm still in my robe and slippers. I'd really like to go fry some bacon (until it is crackly crisp) and a couple of eggs, open some strawberry jam, toast about ten pieces of sourdough bread, and settle down in bed with the new *Good Housekeeping*. Let's see—that would be about . . . sixteen hundred calories! And a wasted morning. And the start of a food binge. Then nausea, then repentance. *Up, woman! Make thy bed, dress, study the Word, eat a correct breakfast. Your self-denial will be rewarded by contentment—and maybe a few ounces lost.*

I want to know Christ and the power of his resurrection and the fellowship of sharing in his sufferings, becoming like him in his death, and . . . to attain to the resurrection from the dead (Phil. 3:10).

I wonder if, when I deny my body's lust for food, I might possibly be sharing a fraction of His sufferings? One time He fasted forty days. Forty days! The thought of fasting two days sends me into despair. When He was forced to carry His own cross, heavy and splintery, through a jeering and hostile mob, when He hung for hours from nail-pierced hands and feet, His mind was set on doing the Father's will, not on His suffering.

My life is safe and easy. I have time to sit around thinking up good foods to buy and eat. I haven't had any experience that would compare to my Savior's agony, but maybe my self-denial will give me a glimpse of His sufferings.

Lord Jesus, Savior, please let today's hunger pangs and my self-denial be a means to know You better. Remind me that I will never have to suffer as You did for me. Remind me also that I have Your resurrection power to forget food.

HOW CAN A NICE
GLAZED DONUT
LIKE YOU BE
SO BAD FOR ME?
SIX TEASPOONS
OF SUGAR? YOU
CAN'T BE SERIOUS!

Waffles, Sweet Rolls, Pancakes

I kept thinking about the devotion yesterday, about the fellowship of sharing Christ's sufferings through hunger pangs. Of course, my small discomfort couldn't be compared with what He suffered, but each time my stomach contracted with hunger I thanked Him for what He did on the cross for me. And to think He suffered for me when He knew I would waste many precious years living like His enemy.

Many live as enemies of the cross of Christ. Their destiny is destruction, their god is their stomach, and their glory is in their shame. Their mind is on earthly things (Phil. 3:18–19).

I was so shocked when I read this verse I decided to reread the whole chapter so I could know whom Paul was talking about. The ones living as enemies of the cross of Christ were not the unsaved, but Christians! His words seem to be a flame of fire as he sneers, "Their god is their stomach!" As I meditate on this verse I see myself sitting in church, hands folded over the Bible, innocent eyes on the pastor, but with my mind, on waffles, sweet rolls, pancakes. . .

Dear Lord Jesus, I don't want my stomach to be my god! Help me this day to rise above earthly things, and keep my heart centered on You.

Soul Food

How I wish I could live yesterday again. How I wish there were some way to make me remember today's regret. How can I be such a failure? I'm always spouting Scripture and singing "Faith is the victory." Yesterday I even prayed I wouldn't be a stomach worshiper—and then I ate like a pagan at an orgy. All this on a Sunday, too.

First we went to Joan's after church, and I didn't feel I was eating too much, although it wasn't exactly health foods: potato chips, macaroni salad, mayonnaise on luncheon meat sandwiches, then birthday cake. Later we went to mom's for an evening "snack." Fried chicken, mashed potatoes and gravy, Jell-O salad, and ice cream. Gleefully I ate. I had to, didn't I? After all, this stuff was *prepared* for us.

Well, I am paying for it. I gained two pounds.

For you have spent enough time in the past doing what pagans choose to do—living in debauchery,

lust, drunkenness, orgies, carousing and detestable
idolatry (1 Peter 4:3).

When Jesus stayed at Zacchaeus' house I'm sure he
didn't overeat, even if Zacchaeus served pecan pie a' la
mode. He was too concerned for Zacchaeus' soul to pay
attention to food.

Was I concerned for anyone's soul yesterday? Of course
not. I was too occupied with how good everything tasted to
think about Jesus—in terms of myself or anyone else.
When will I learn to listen to Him all the time, even on
Sunday?

Lord, I can't look at You today. I'm always asking for
Your help, which You always give. But what good does
asking for help do me, if I won't accept it?

Battle of the Brain

I feel humbled this morning, but hopeful. I know the dear Lord forgives, even gluttony. He is always ready to begin again with me.

I have lost one of those awful pounds I put on over the weekend. I've learned a hard lesson . . . I think. Although family or friends may pressure me to eat foods not in the plan, I still have the option to say either "yes, please" or "no thanks." It is up to me to "program" my brain to say "no thanks" and not change discs!

Whatever is true, whatever is noble, whatever is right, whatever is pure, whatever is lovely, whatever is admirable—if anything is excellent or praiseworthy—think about such things (Phil. 4:8).

The battle of the bulge is really a battle of the brain. I may think my thoughts are centered on a certain thing, but then I realize a corner of my tricky brain is off on something it shouldn't be. For example: even now, part of my brain is remorseful and ashamed of the recent binge, but another part of my brain is at the refrigerator door. Why? Because last night my friend gave me a piece of cheesecake to sample, and there it sits: right on the top shelf. Deceitful brain! Whatever is true, noble, right, pure, lovely, admirable, excellent, praiseworthy—think about these things.

As I think about these things I discover that *Christ alone* is true, noble, right, pure, lovely, admirable, excellent, and worthy of all my praise!

Father, program my brain today to think Jesus.

Paul Paunchy?

There is power in the name of Jesus. The Bible says that at the name of Jesus every knee should bow (Phil. 2:10). That includes my knee and also Satan's! Yesterday, every time I thought *food,* I whispered, "Jesus." It worked! I even ground up the cheesecake in the garbage disposal. (Nobody else needed that fat, either.)

You are witnesses, and so is God, of how holy, righteous and blameless we were among you who believed.... Encouraging, comforting and urging you to live lives worthy of God (1 Thess. 2:10, 12).

A niece asked me how I could find so many verses in the Bible to use for weight control. I told her the more I study the Word, the more I realize my outward appearance is a reflection of my inward state. So the more I grow like Christ on the inside, the better I will look on the outside. In that case, *all* the Bible verses in regard to righteous living can be applied to weight control. I can't imagine Paul or Peter—or any of the apostles—with stomachs hanging over their girdles! In the verse above Paul urged Christians to live lives worthy of God. If Paul had been overweight and paunchy, the Thessalonian Christians would have laughed at him. Excessive fat is usually evidence of gluttony and disobedience. *Oh, Mab, beware, beware. When you die you don't want to be issued size forty wings, do you?*

Dear Jesus, I want to be slender not only for myself and Joe, but for the testimony before family, friends, and strangers.

Feeling Pretty

I feel pretty—Oh so pretty—I feel pretty, and witty, and. . .

I *do* feel pretty! Well, at least prettier. I've lost another pound. I feel not only prettier, but healthier and more ambitious. Today, I'm going to clean the oven and mop the kitchen floor, then straighten up the house. After that, I'll call Joan and see if she'll meet me for lunch. I feel like celebrating!

We instructed you how to live in order to please God, as in fact you are living. Now we ask you and urge you in the Lord Jesus to do this more and more (1 Thess. 4:1).

Rats. Did I *have* to find that verse this morning? . . . "*Urge* you in the Lord Jesus to do this more and more." *In other words, kiddo, just stay on your calorie count and don't go running to the pizza palace to celebrate.*

Now that I'm over the disappointment, I'm glad I read this Scripture today. I was so happy when I saw I had lost weight that I felt I *deserved* something fattening. As a child of God, however, I *deserve* to treat my body better than that. Finding this verse, today, when I was on the verge of a splurge, fills me with awe. God really cares. He wants me to rely on Him more and more, continually.

Dear Lord, thank You for caring. Thank You for re-newing my resolve. Please continue to protect me from my own appetite.

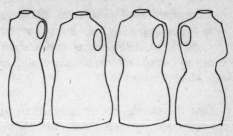

Doing It My Way

Barbara called. She's also having a problem with her weight. Seems everyone I know is struggling with the "fat monster." We shared some things that help. She told me she often eats a whole cucumber (twenty-five calories) for a snack. It satisfies her urge to chew and makes her stomach feel full. I'll have to remember to buy cucumbers. She sometimes drinks a cup of almost boiling water, sipping it like coffee. Satisfying, she said, and much better for the body than tea or coffee. I told her I always find relief in prayer, *if* I take time to concentrate on the person of Christ. We agreed we both feel much, much better when we are losing weight—and not eating junk.

For God did not call us to be impure, but to live a holy life. Therefore, he who rejects this instruction does not reject man but God (1 Thess. 4:7–8).

This portion was written in regard to sex sins, but to God, sin is sin. In the Word He tells us that overeating is sin. So when I stuff myself with "choice goodies" I am not only acting impurely, but I am full of impurities.

I wish I could remember that Jesus didn't die on the cross so I would be free to sit and stuff, but so I could rise and shine for Him.

Dear heavenly Father, I want to apologize for the times I have rejected Your instructions. I would never purposely reject You! But the verse states I already have. Forgive me.

Stay at Home

Sipping hot water, Barbara style, didn't tantalize my taste buds, but it kept my hands busy and made me feel pretty full. Who knows? Maybe in time I will like it as well as coffee. I haven't lost any weight, though, for days. I don't know why, because I am counting calories scrupulously. What am I doing wrong?

Make it your ambition to lead a quiet life, to mind your own business and to work with your hands (1 Thess. 4:11).

This verse seems to contradict itself. To me ambition always has involved being up and doing, so how can ambition have anything to do with being quiet? Maybe this verse is the key to why I haven't lost weight lately. My life is anything but quiet. I have so much running around to do that a whole day at home is a luxury. At least two days a week I have to go somewhere for lunch, sometimes it's business and sometimes, pleasure. Before I go to a restaurant, I always decide what I will order. That helps. But I never know what's in the dishes. I'm convinced restaurant food has more calories than the same food prepared by me—at home. In fact, I've noticed every time I order a chef's salad, I gain! When I told Rhea that, she suggested I order salad dressing on the side. "Then," she said, "you can control how much you put on." Good advice, but I still wish I could stay home more.

How can I lead a quieter life? If I could eliminate some of my duties outside the home, I wouldn't have to go to so many luncheons. It's really hard not to eat food when it's placed before you. That verse also says to "mind your own business." If I stayed home more, I could. I could get my yard work caught up and at the same time burn off calories. A dieter's paraphrase of 1 Thessalonians 4:11 could be: Try hard to stay at home; fix your own lunch; and get your work done.

Lord Jesus, thank You for personalizing this verse. Help me put it into practice.

Don't Ask Me

Sis gave me a tip on how I could cut back on my church and school responsibilities. She said, "Remember when I was teaching kindergarten everyday?" I nodded. "Well, I was also singing in the choir, serving as Sunday school superintendent and librarian. I was so frazzled, yet I was afraid to say no to anyone who asked me to do something for fear I might be turning down a job the Lord had earmarked for me."

"I know! That's how I feel."

"Finally, I prayed the Lord wouldn't let anyone ask me to do anything unless it was His direct will!"

"Did it work?"

"Yes! Nobody approached me for months. In fact, one of my friends volunteered to take over the library for me."

I prayed that way this morning. I told the Lord I really wanted to serve Him, but asked for His help in cutting out some of the purely social, time-wasting activities. If I were home more, my house would look better, and the temptation to overeat, or eat foods I shouldn't, would be lessened.

Be joyful always; pray continually; give thanks in all circumstances, for this is God's will for you in Christ Jesus (1 Thess. 5:16–18).

This verse tells me plainly that whether I am at home, at a meeting, or anywhere, I am to be joyful! No more feeling sorry for myself because I can't have a hot fudge sundae with the rest of the gang. I must be thankful for the good foods I *may* eat—and for how much better my clothes fit. (That alone should make me joyful!)

But pray *continually?* How can I? I can't, but the Holy Spirit can. Romans 8:26 says the Spirit helps us pray with words we can't express. I must remember to invite Him to take over in prayer.

What about giving thanks in *all* circumstances? What if Joe loses his job? Or I'm asked to take junior church? Or if I gain a pound?

This Scripture is not easy.

Dear Holy Spirit, You alone can make me joyful and thankful all the time. You alone can pray continually. Please help me obey this verse.

Eve, Food, and Me

The car gave me an opportunity to see how well I had learned to be joyful and thankful. I had planned to have lunch with Rhea (a date I made a month ago), then do the week's grocery shopping but, when I turned on the ignition, the battery was dead. My first impulse was anger, but I made myself say out loud, "Lord, I don't feel joyful or thankful, but I'm trying."

All anger left me!

I went back in the house, called Rhea. changed clothes, and worked in the yard. It was a wonderful day—and I just now thought of this: Maybe the Lord used this situation to answer my prayer about staying home! The only bad thing is I have to buy groceries today.

The eye is the lamp of the body. If your eyes are good, your whole body will be full of light. But if your eyes are bad, your whole body will be full of darkness (Matt. 6:22–23).

When Jesus said this He was referring to the futility of storing up treasure on earth. If our spiritual eyes can look at money and what it will buy without worshiping it, great. But if we let riches become our god, then our lives will be dark and sad.

However, when I read this verse, I thought of Eve, food, and me. When Eve saw the forbidden fruit, it looked so good she wanted to eat it. She wanted it so much she decided to disobey God. Through her disobedience she really messed up God's perfect plan for her life—and everybody else's too.

Today I have to buy groceries. I praise God that I'm not blind, that I have two good eyes and am able to see everything; but I also know these eyes will see shelves full of candy bars, cakes, pies, potato chips, Fritos (I figured out *one* Frito is twelve calories), and ice cream. I'll need God's strength to pass by the junk which looks so good (while feeling joyful and thankful of course), and stock up on milk, cottage cheese, whole grain cereals, bread, fresh fruit, vegetables, fish, chicken, and beef.

Oh, God! Put blinders on me as I go through the bakery section. Make my eyes spiritually good, so my body won't be full of darkness.

Left Face

At the market I learned something amazing about God. Before I started the food program, I always spent a lot of shopping time in the bakery section, looking, smelling, drooling, and, finally, buying. But as I entered the market, I remembered the verse about "good eyes" and whispered, "Lord, help me not to look." When I walked down that aisle of wonderful sights and smells, I turned my face slightly to the left so I couldn't see the donuts, cakes, and cookies. People probably thought I had a stiff neck as I hurried along, but I learned that the moment I prayed and turned my face away from temptation, God took over! I had no hunger pangs, no desire to look back. The rest of the shopping was easy, and there is nothing on my shelves this morning that shouldn't be. And now for today's battle!

If a man will not work, he shall not eat. We hear that some among you are idle. They are not busy; they are busybodies (2 Thess. 3:10–11).

God is pretty emphatic about not being lazy. He knows I will be happier, my body will function better, and my mind will be clearer if I keep busy. Although I don't have a salaried job at present, I still have hard work at home for which I am responsible. The days I am lazy and want to lie around and read, or wander in and out of the kitchen in search of another snack, or talk on the phone (busybody!), I don't feel good, am not happy, and usually end up feeling remorseful for wasting time. Often, on those lazy days, someone comes over and finds my house a mess. Then I'm not only remorseful, but ashamed. I've discovered something else about those lazy days—even if I stay within the calorie count, I usually don't lose. No exercise. Self-discipline and physical exertion go hand-in-hand to produce weight loss.

Thank You, Lord, for these verses. I'm going to work hard today!

OH, NO! THIS PIECE OF CAKE HAS FIFTEEN TEA-SPOONS OF SUGAR IN IT?

Birthday Pig Out

We had a birthday party here for mom yesterday. The whole family came. Following our custom, each household brought something special, so of course the table was laden with food, all of it tempting. Pat brought her sticky rolls, delicious sweet bread, chock-full of raisins and nuts; Bobbie brought candy, thick, caramel chunks, full of almonds and pecans and coated with milk chocolate. Someone had given Joe a two-pound box of See's chocolates, so we figured we would share them with the whole family. Then there was the birthday cake, a big, beautiful creation I bought. I felt guilty at the time, but, after all, she's only eighty-two once, and a birthday cake is an important tradition. Besides all that, we had hamburgers, baked beans, dips, chips, fruit, pistachio pudding, Jell-O (Oh, not plain—no! Full of nuts, coconut, bananas, tangerines. . .).

I withstood temptation for about an hour, but finally ate one of the chocolates. I sincerely wished I hadn't. It was so sweet and gooey I really didn't want to swallow it. I was also terribly tempted by some of Pat's sticky rolls and finally did eat a few raisins and nuts which had fallen to the plate, but God gave me the power to get away from it. Later, while everyone else was pigging out, I didn't feel deprived or tempted. I know it's because I took time for personal devotions early in the morning: He came to my rescue.

Train yourself to be godly. For physical training is of some value, but godliness has value for all things, holding promise for both the present life and the life to come (1 Tim. 4:7–8).

What an appropriate Scripture for me this morning. "Train yourself to be godly." How? By studying the Bible and putting it into practice. God is telling me to keep on studying the Word every morning, and, although physical exercise is important, I am also to keep on asking for His help. (What a thought! I am not only growing thinner, but I am growing bigger in the Lord!) These morning devotions are so sweet and strengthening. I know if I continue these moments with Jesus, I will be able to eat properly all the rest of my life and never go back to binging. Of equal importance, I am learning more everyday about my future home (heaven) and its master, my *Lord.*

All praise to You, Lord, for getting me started on "diet devotions."

Waist Not

Our refrigerator is full of delicious leftovers and I don't know what to do with them. I tried to make everyone take home what was left, but that didn't work. So now pistachio pudding, potato chips, half a box of chocolates, jazzed-up Jell-O, and half the bakery cake (which turned out to be *awful*) sit in my kitchen. What should I do? All my life I've been taught, "Waste not, want not." But under the present circumstances would it be wrong to throw it all away? I *know* me. If I keep looking at all that stuff I'll weaken.

Be strong in the grace that is in Christ Jesus. ... Endure hardship with us like a good soldier of Christ Jesus. No one serving as a soldier gets involved in civilian affairs—he wants to please his commanding officer (2 Tim. 2:1, 3–4).

What a perfect answer! Feeling thin is so wonderful! I don't ever want to go back. The only way to keep that fat

77

off is to *be strong.* But how? By doing all in my power to fight the enemy (fat). So, should I make friends with the enemy's allies (candy, cake, junk)? No! I am to endure hardship like a good soldier. And what does that mean? It means continuing to deny myself certain foods that are bad for me. Enduring hardship means I am not to think about yesterday's goodies, but to step back in line as a good soldier of Christ, so as to please my commanding officer.

Lord, I am weak, but You are strong. I pledge my allegiance to You again this morning. Give me the strength to do something with all these leftovers— anything except eat them.

Down the Drain

I did it! Right or wrong, I did it! I threw away the pudding, Jell-O, and that awful cake. Yes, I know three-fourths of the world goes hungry each night. I feel sad and guilty about it, but there's no way I could get that food to them (it wouldn't be good for them if I could), and if it stays in my refrigerator, I'll be the one who eats it. The See's chocolates are something else. Since they were given to Joe, they aren't mine to throw away—so I put the box in the freezer. First, though, I put it in a plastic bag and sealed it with tape. It's no trick for me to eat chocolates when they are frozen solid.

Therefore I endure everything for the sake of the elect, that they too may obtain the salvation that is in Christ Jesus, with eternal glory (2 Tim. 2:10).

This is a strong reminder that I must keep my weight down if anyone is going to believe me when I say I want to bring glory to Christ. If I cannot find help from my God to handle my problems and lack of willpower, how can I expect others, who don't know Jesus, to call on Him to save *their* bodies? As I learned yesterday, endure means to *hold out against*—against what? A "bite" of donut, one french fry, a chocolate? Jesus *endured* the cross so I could escape eternal punishment. Can't I endure a few hunger pangs, a little pressure from loved ones, some discomfort, so others will believe Christ is real in my life? Through God's grace I can. However, it doesn't hurt to get rid of temptation.

Jesus, thank You for giving me grace to throw out the unwholesome food. Give me endurance, Your kind of endurance—cross-endurance.

THIS IS INCREDIBLE.
ONE TEASPOON OF SUGAR IN
JUST ONE TEASPOON
OF JELLY
OR
JAM
?!

Toast—M-m-m Good

I was thrilled yesterday when my neighbor Peggy and I got to talking, first about diets, then the Lord. Tears came to her eyes when she said, "I'm just miserable! I've got to do something about my weight, but nothing works!" She is a bit chubby and needs to get rid of a few pounds. I told her about the book and how I study and pray every morning. She seemed impressed, especially when I told her how much weight I've lost. I told her I'd be praying for her, and suggested we might meet a couple of times a week for mutual encouragement. She accepted Jesus Christ as her own Savior several years ago, but with a husband who has to work Sundays, and two babies she has sort of left God out of her life. Now I know when Joe and I found this house, God had Peggy in mind. How exciting!

But you, keep your head in all situations, endure hardship, do the work of an evangelist, discharge all the duties of your ministry (2 Tim. 4:5).

"Keep your head in all situations." In other words, if several of us go out after evening church for a treat, and everyone around me orders a hot fudge sundae, I am to keep in mind the things I've learned: the sad times when I have eaten too much, how it hurts to get on the scales and see a gain, how awful it feels to be nauseated from *stuffing* myself. I am to remember to call on the Lord for help to choose the right kind of treat. Such as? Such as whole wheat toast and a glass of milk. To me, nothing is as satisfying as toast. Or I could order a salad entree or cottage cheese and a peach. The fellowship would be just as sweet, with no regrets in the morning. That is the meaning of "keep your head" and "endure hardship"—at least, for me.

But how can I do the work of an evangelist? I always thought that involved being a preacher who traveled around trying to start revivals, but the dictionary says an evangelist is first of all, a preacher of the gospel. He or she tells the story of Christ's birth, death, and resurrection— His life and victorious suffering which paid for all our sins. So, according to this verse, *I* am also to preach the gospel, every chance I get. I'm glad I talked about Jesus to Peggy, but with her it was easy because she is a Christian. How can I go about being an evangelist to the other neighbors?

Dear Lord, help me to "discharge" all my duties. Help me to be a genuine reflector of Your love.

Billy Graham I'm Not

Being a neighborhood evangelist isn't so easy. I have prayed for an opening to witness to the older couple next door. This morning I was watering the front lawn when the woman came outside. I smiled and waved. "Good morning," I called. "How are you today?"

She shrugged and smiled.

I said, "Boy, these weeds sure come up fast, don't they?"

She shrugged and smiled.

I sprinkled a little more. "Do you have any children?" I tried again.

She shrugged and smiled, then, "No spik so gutt."

It was my turn to smile and shrug. I don't know what to do—but the Lord does.

Then Jesus declared, "I am the bread of life. He who comes to me will never go hungry, and he who believes in me will never be thirsty" (John 6:35).

This could be the best verse I've found! I realize Jesus is talking about salvation and spiritual hunger. But it's still true in every area of life. Jesus *is* satisfying. Today I'm going to put this verse to the test. I'm going to write Jesus' words, "He who comes to me will never go hungry," on a card and tape it on the refrigerator door. Then every time I start to open the door, I'll pause and say, "Jesus, I'm coming to You—take away my hunger." He will do it! When I count the pounds I've lost—more than on any other diet—I *know* it's by the power of Christ.

When morning gilds the skies,
My heart awaking cries:
May Jesus Christ be praised.

—Translated by
Edward Caswall

Off With the Old

Scripture on the refrigerator door is great! Twice I went to get something to eat, but both times I read Jesus' promise, called out to Him, then walked away. Some might say it was purely psychological. Maybe so, but it still worked—because Jesus has power over my psyche!

You were taught, with regard to your former way of life, to put off your old self . . . and to put on the new self, created to be like God (Eph. 44:22, 24).

The old self and the new self—villain and hero in the food drama. Satan wants me fat to dishonor God and thereby cripple my service for the kingdom; God wants me to be just right, so I'll not only look good, but feel good, in order to bring Him glory. As long as I live I'll be saddled with the two natures. Whichever nature I feed will be the strongest. That's why it is so important for me to take time for these meditations, because I receive power and motivation from the Bible. On the other hand, the days I wander around, sit and watch talk shows or soaps, I become discontented, and want to complain, and, worst of all, I want to *eat.* John 8:44 says Satan is a liar and a murderer. All my adult life he has tried to kill me, first with his lies about drinking alcohol, and then with lies about the satisfaction of gorging. I'm a Christian now, but if I feed on trashy TV programs, bad books, and poor music, I lose my battle with Satan and overeat. But if I feed on Bible reading, prayer, and listening to good music, then, through Christ I win the battle against overeating. When I ask Christ to protect me, the battle is over.

Help me Jesus, to hide in You, and to be like You today.

Heel!

Yesterday morning Satan must have been reading over my shoulder. He evidently didn't like what he saw, because he yanked the rug out from under me. When comedian Flip Wilson used to say, "The Devil made me do it!" I would laugh, but it doesn't seem funny this morning. In fact, I feel like crying. I was *certain* another pound would be gone, but instead I gained half a pound! I guess I was careless about counting calories. Today I will be on guard, with the belt of truth pulled tightly around my waist, and my ears turned only to God.

If this man were not from God he could do nothing (John 9:33).

Jesus made a blind man see! Think of it. I can understand what a great miracle that was, because, for the past year of mother's life, cataracts almost blinded her. It was pitiful to see her walk into walls, speak to lamps, and put her cup down in space. We prayed for a miracle, for the return of her sight. I can imagine this man's excitement—seeing for the very first time. No wonder he told the Pharisees Jesus was from God. It thrills and amazes me that the power which opened this blind man's eyes is living *inside* me! How can I fail at anything I do?

Why did I fail yesterday? I just blamed Satan, but I know that isn't the whole truth. After my morning devotions, I did not go to Jesus again the rest of the day. True, Satan may have kept me so busy with phone calls, watering, and housework that I didn't bother to look up calories or pray or think about what I had learned. Still, it was my fault for not taking time to get on my knees, look into His face, and receive His help for the day.

O, Lord, I feel as ugly as a mongrel with the mange. Put me on Your leash today, and, when I think I have to have a snack, just give my head a good jerk.

Absent and Present

As I found out before, this battle of losing weight is in the mind. I proved it again yesterday. I volunteered to hang paper in one of the restrooms at church, so before I left home I ate a proper, food-plan breakfast. I didn't think it would take long to paper a little bathroom, so I didn't take a lunch. However, I worked until three o'clock. Completely absorbed in the task at hand, I didn't even take time to cross the street to get a hamburger. I couldn't believe it was four o'clock when I got home, and I still wasn't hungry! The restroom looked good—and so did the scales this morning. Another pound vanished into the atmosphere!

As long as we are at home in the body we are away from the Lord.... We are confident, I say, and would prefer to be away from the body and at home with the Lord. So we make it our goal to please him, whether we are at home in the body or away from it (2 Cor. 5:6, 8–9).

When Paul wrote this he was referring to physical death. It's obvious that while we are alive in these bodies, we're not with the Lord in heaven. But I thought of this in another way. When I am "at home" in my body, comfortable, self-centered, eating anything I want with no discipline, I am absent from the Lord! This is *true*. It has happened to me over and over; when I indulge my physical appetites, I become spiritually cold. When *I* occupy, God is left outside.

Am I willing, *this* day, as Paul was, to be away from the body, that is to leave the comfort of stuffing myself, in order to be at home with, in fellowship with, the Lord? Is it really my goal to please Christ?

Right this minute, Lord, I say yes. Please help me to be "tough" with my body all day.

Not So Fast

I felt victorious yesterday. No guess-timating on the calorie counting and no standing at the refrigerator door. That verse, "He who comes to me will never go hungry," is still working. Mother was in my thoughts a lot yesterday, too. Even in her nineties, she still had a good figure. She always told Sis and me not to go on fad diets (we did anyway), but to eat sensibly. "Honey, you can have anything you want, if you'll only practice moderation." If only I had obeyed mother all these years, I wouldn't have to be dieting today. Children, obey your parents!

For our light and momentary troubles are achieving for us an eternal glory that far outweighs them all. So we fix our eyes not on what is seen, but on what is unseen. For what is seen is temporary, but what is unseen is eternal (2 Cor. 4:17–18).

What a comfort the Bible verse is today. Not often, but sometimes, I feel deprived, sorry for myself, especially about chocolate. When I first started this plan I intended to stay with it only until I could get my weight down—I estimated a few weeks. (Once, on a fad diet, I lost eight pounds in eight days.) But this weight hasn't come off that fast. I've been having "diet devotions" for nine months—long enough to have a baby! (I feel as slender as if I'd had one, too!) If I had always stayed within my calorie limit, I would have had quicker results. But I shouldn't complain, because the private times of study and meditation have thrilled me, strengthened me, renewed my faith and desire to see heaven. I really want to see Jesus face to face. With this in mind, I can understand when it says there is an eternal glory in store for me in heaven, which far outweighs any frustration or disappointment I have experienced on this earth.

Thank You, Father, for encouraging me, for causing me to look up to what is eternal, instead of keeping my eyes on temporal things.

HMM. DO I REALLY NEED THE EIGHT TEASPOONS OF SUGAR IN THIS CHOCOLATE CANDY BAR ?

Chocoholic

Sometimes I feel so close to the Lord. At times He is all-important to me, above my husband or children. Other times, like today, thoughts of Jesus are vague. I can't recapture the feeling I had yesterday, the yearning to see Him. All I can think about is the mountain of dirty laundry, how old I am getting, and that I don't care if I get fat. I do not want to read the Bible. I would like to eat a piece of chocolate cake, with thick, chocolate icing. Oh me. I guess that's positive proof I had better read the Bible.

For we must all appear before the judgment seat of Christ, that each one may receive what is due him for the things done while in the body, whether good or bad (2 Cor. 5:10).

Heavy! It never before occurred to me that Christ will not only judge me, but will judge me for what I've put in my body! What will He say about all the chocolate I've eaten?

For years I've known that chocolate is difficult to digest and constipating. Eating it is almost as hard on the body as eating mud would be. Yet knowing this, I have continued to eat large amounts of chocolate, year after year. If all the hot fudge sundaes I've eaten were poured together, how big a container would be filled? A garbage can? A wading pool? Ugh. What a revolting thought. And I wonder how many pounds of sugar have I forced my poor body to digest? May God have mercy on me!

Heavenly Father, forgive me for abusing my digestive system. Forgive me for hating my body and forcing it to handle undigestible foods. Make me willing to be willing to give up chocolate, not for a few weeks, but forever.

Built-in Tiger

Last night at Bible study the refreshments were big, fudgie cookies (of course). I can't believe I did it, but I turned them down! I drank my unsweetened herbal tea and felt happy and a teensy bit smug as others put that gook in their stomachs. The plate came around a second time, and when it got to me there was half a cookie left. I looked at it, looked away, then ate it. Oh rats! I can't live for Christ even one day.

I know what my problem is. I am not totally convinced that eating chocolate, sweets, or even overeating is all that bad, much less sin. I don't know if I am glossing it over, or if I haven't really faced it. I was doing so well, for awhile, but the closer I get to my goal the harder it is to stay with the program. Most mornings I have been thrilled with the Scriptures, and in my heart I know I love the Lord; but this flesh of mine is like a hungry tiger, always ready to break out of the cage of discipline and gobble everything in sight. And *I* am the one who opens the door.

*God made him who had no sin to be sin for us, so
that in him we might become the righteousness of
God (2 Cor. 5:21).*

I know the things I was doing before I accepted Christ
were *sin.* When I first heard that Christ died for those sins, I
readily acknowledged them and gratefully accepted Him
as my Savior. The main sin that brought me to the Cross
was overindulgence in alcohol. Without an argument, I
knew that was wrong. Proverbs 23:20 says: "Do not join
those who drink too much wine or gorge themselves."

So there it is, once and for all. God lumps the two together. I wouldn't think of going back to drinking. God
forbid! So am I closing my eyes to sin when I gorge? I've
got to recognize that overindulgence in anything is wrong.
Participating in food orgies (even at church!), helping to
plan unhealthy dinners, or offering junk foods to my loved
ones is sin. As long as I overeat or poison my body with
chemical additives, I shall not become the righteousness
of God.

*O righteous God, make me stern with myself, so that I
can become the righteous person You want me to be.*

Chew—Chew

Some of the teenagers were at our house Friday night. I baked a turkey and sweet potatoes, cooked green beans, and made a huge salad. For dessert I baked a plain cake. (I didn't think the boys would understand if I didn't serve something for dessert.) During dinner I watched how the skinny, lovely girls ate. Hardly at all! I watched Michelle especially. I wonder if she has anorexia. She would pick up a tiny morsel on her fork, laugh, talk, finally put it in her mouth, put the fork down, chew *forever* before she swallowed, laugh some more, ask questions, drink water, and play with her napkin. Although she put small portions of everything on her plate, she scarcely touched anything. In fact, most of the girls left a lot of food on their plates. It irritated me—I had worked hard on the meal, the food was delicious, and I don't believe in wasting food. But I learned something. If a person takes tiny bites, chews a long time, is interested in others, rather than how to fill the cavity, then ones does not eat much.

Do not be yoked together with unbelievers. . . .
What fellowship can light have with darkness?
What harmony is there between Christ and Belial?"
(2 Cor. 6:14–15).

When I became a Christian, this truth was pointed out to me, and it didn't take long to break off with all the worldly couples with whom we had been partying. I knew if I was to succeed in the Christian life I couldn't take the chance of being pulled back down into old habits.

Today I see this also applies to my food-life. Although most of my friends now are Christians and our fellowship is Christ-oriented, we eat too much. Almost every business meeting at church or women's missionary meeting is either preceded or followed by dinners or refreshments. Some of the most delicious food in the world is prepared and served at church. What can I do? I should paraphrase it to read: Do not be yoked together with overeaters. . . . What fellowship can the dieter have with the compulsive eater? What harmony is there between Christ and gluttony?

But I want to be with my Christian friends, even if some of them don't understand why I won't eat dessert. I guess I could avoid dinners and only attend the meetings. That won't completely solve the problem, though. Only as I turn my life over to Christ, meal after meal, can I keep from overeating with overeaters.

Help me, dear Lord, to be strong enough to turn away from the super smorgasbords at church. Give me will power to take tiny bites—and chew and chew.

I HEREBY RESOLVE TO WALK AWAY FROM THAT SMOOTH CREAMY SCOOP OF ICE CREAM. I JUST LEARNED IT HAS FOUR TEASPOONS OF SUGAR.

Appetite Is Appetite

One of the women at church is so heavy she has to make most of her clothes. She isn't well, either. She has diabetes, gout, and headaches.

"I know I'm too fat," she sighed one day, "but I can't help it."

This seemed like a good opening to tell her about the food plan, so I said, "I've lost quite a bit of weight on a new program . . ."

"You? You're not fat!"

"You didn't know me last winter! I have to watch it, and on this plan. . ."

"Hah!" she snorted. "You *couldn't* know what it means to have to watch it! You're probably never really hungry!" With that she moved away.

Maybe I don't weigh as much as she does, but I know my animal appetite is just as fierce as hers.

Keep me safe, O, God, for in you I take refuge. I have set the Lord always before me. Because he is

at my right hand, I will not be shaken. Therefore
my heart is glad and my tongue rejoices; my body
also will rest secure (Ps. 16:1, 8–9).

If I take refuge in the Lord, He will keep me safe (eating right). If I fail to turn to Him, I will overeat. Like the psalmist, I must set the Lord before me. How can I do that? By prayer. "Lord, You go before me. What groceries shall I buy? Which restaurant should I choose? What should I order? How much may I eat?" Not only must I have the Lord before me, but He must be at all times—always— while I plan and prepare meals and especially after meals, when I've eaten my calorie allowance. Then I need Him to keep me from "tastes" as I do the dishes.

The psalmist also said that God was at his right hand. Mine too! And I do almost everything with my right hand. With God as close as my hand, surely I can say, "I will not be shaken," even when someone tells me I don't need to lose weight.

Wonderful God! My heart is glad and my tongue re-
joices. Lord, I pray for my friend at church. I want her to
be happy, too. I'll be glad to encourage her to start the
food program . . . if You will open the door.

Infinite Insulation

Joe gave me a ruby ring for Christmas a couple of years ago, and though I'm not supposed to love inanimate objects, I *do* love it. I wear it on my right hand all the time. This morning I was looking at it in the sunlight, and, after all this time, it still doesn't have a scratch on it. As I turned my hand this way and that to catch the light, I remembered the verses from yesterday's devotion: "The Lord is at my right hand!" He is as close as the ruby, and that gave me an idea. Today when I start to eat something I shouldn't, I'll see the ring, think of God being right there, and put the food back. Childish? I suppose so—but it's a jewel of a thought to me.

The word of the Lord *is flawless. He is a shield for all who take refuge in him.... Who is the Rock except our God? It is God who arms me with strength* (Ps. 18:30–32).

101

In Bible times a shield was part of a soldier's armor. Although they are no longer G.I. issue, the astronauts still have to have them. If they weren't protected by a heat shield, they would burn up during re-entry. I need a similar shield. When I study the Bible, pray, and meditate, I feel as if I'm up in the heavens—close to God. But when I start on the daily "earthly" activities, I need protection from the burning temptations all around, especially in the area of food. I can't be my shield, but I can hide behind God, who is as impenetrable as a mountain of granite.

In these verses the psalmist also declares the Word of God (the Bible) flawless. My little ruby is flawless. That's the reason it reflects the sunlight so brilliantly. In fact, its tiny rays are almost blinding. It's that way with God's Word. It is an exact reflection of Jesus Christ, and I can count on it being absolute truth.

Thank You, Lord, for being flawless, for being my Shield, my Rock, my Strength, for being as close as my right hand.

Flaming Arrows

The lady across the street came over while I was pruning the roses.

"Have you been sick?" she asked.

"No! Why?"

"Well . . . I haven't seen you for a few days. And . . . your face is so thin!"

Gr-rr! I *know* my face gets thin when I lose weight. So do my bust and legs. But that old stomach hangs in there—or, rather, hangs out there. Her remark really discouraged me. I don't want to look sick. There's no getting around it, my face looks better when I'm heavier. For about thirty seconds I considered putting away the nippers and racing down to Winchell's for donuts. But I handed her a rosebud and went in the house.

When I sat down to have morning devotions, the Lord reminded me about the armor of God and Satan's fiery darts. I turned to the Book of Ephesians.

*Put on the full armor of God so that you can take
your stand against the devil's schemes. For our
struggle is not against flesh and blood, but against
the rulers, against the authorities, against the pow-
ers of this dark world (Eph. 6:11–12).*

After Bible study I realized I hadn't taken early morning
time to put on the armor. I had forgotten all about hiding
behind the Rock. I had been anxious to work on the roses
before it got hot.

I am convinced I must have early morning devotions,
before I get started on anything, or else the day doesn't go
well. I've proved it several times. When I don't have a quiet
time first, I either overeat or am lazy or get my feelings
hurt. Satan knew exactly how to stab me with his flaming
arrow—through pride and vanity. It hurt when my neighbor said my face was thin. (She might as well have added
wrinkled.)

The verses above say my struggle to lose weight isn't
against flesh and blood, but against Satan and his host of
unholy angels, unseen adversaries who think up fantastic
schemes to get me discouraged.

*Jesus, I want to thank You for bringing to my mind
Ephesians 6 and for showing me that, as long as I am
inside Your armor, I can take my stand against Satan.*

Peace

Joe has just gone to work, and it's a beautiful morning. A perfect morning to weed, fertilize, and spray the flower beds. But no you don't, Satan. *This* morning the Bible and prayer come first!

> *Grace and peace to you from God our Father and the Lord Jesus Christ, who gave himself for our sins to rescue us from the present evil age, according to the will of our God and Father, to whom be glory for ever and ever (Gal. 1:3–5).*

God wants me to have peace. This gift is mine because Jesus gave Himself for my sins. But what's wrong? I'm not always peaceful. Today I seem to remember only the restless days. When I was too fat I never had peace; I continually worried about my gaining. Now I've almost reached my goal, and I keep worrying I'll gain the weight back! Where is my peace? If it's my gift, I want it! The answer has to be faith in Christ. He gave Himself for me in order to rescue me from this present evil age (which included high calorie, worthless food). According to the dictionary, rescue means to free, deliver, or liberate. When someone is held hostage in a foreign land, he or she has to eat whatever the captors provide, no matter how distasteful. But when rescued and taken home, the free person can eat whatever he or she wants. I was a hostage before I became a Christian. Jesus died for me and rescued me from the Prince of this world. Because I am no longer his prisoner, I no longer have to eat the foods of this present evil age. I have been liberated, set free to enjoy the Lord's bounteous table. Why, as though still a prisoner, would I even consider eating Satan's fare?

"You will keep in perfect peace him whose mind . . . trusts in you." (Isa. 26:3).

Jesus, keep my mind on You; then I will have constant peace.

Page One

We've had company for the past three days, and in that time, I haven't kept my rendezvous with the Lord or counted calories. I tried to estimate a few times—the Lord stayed at my right hand, warning, warning, warning! Sometimes I obeyed Him, sometimes not. It's hard to think about eating correctly when I'm on the go, eating at restaurants, snacking late at night, and especially when everyone else is stuffing. But all this undisciplined eating took its toll. When I stepped on the scale this morning I had gained *two* pounds. I felt like having a fit! I wanted to chuck the whole food plan, and eat, eat, eat! But I know from the past—eating would make me more miserable than ever. I know the only road to victory is through Jesus. So, back to page one.

Those who trust in the LORD are like Mount Zion, which cannot be shaken but endures forever. As the mountains surround Jerusalem, so the LORD surrounds his people (Ps. 125:1–2).

If I trust in God, I put my life in His hands. I haven't been trusting him these past three days. Instead of getting up early in order to read the Bible, I've slept as late as my guests. Every morning I've cooked bacon, eggs, and toast —and served sweet rolls besides. Right after breakfast we've gone sightseeing, and, of course, eaten junk foods for lunch. Our evening meals have been gourmet feasts, because everyone wanted to buy someting to contribute. Orgies!

They're gone this morning, and I'm trying to let the Scriptures sink in. *The Lord surrounds me.* All I can think of is the leftovers that surround me. Didn't I come to the place where I truly believed sugars and fats were the enemy? Then why was I so easily shaken from the plan?

Because I did not trust the Lord. I did not put my life in His hands.

There is one bright spot. I did not eat any chocolate! That is a victory and a sign of some progress.

Heavenly Father, I'm ashamed to face You today. Forgive me for not taking the time to trust in You. If only I had taken time for "intake instructions," I wouldn't have gained. Lord, I'm afraid to promise You I will never overeat again, because I have failed before. But I am so heartbroken and discouraged, I don't believe I'll forget this sad day. Give me courage to start over.

TWENTY!
DID YOU SAY
TWENTY
TEASPOONS
OF SUGAR IN
A MILKSHAKE?

Dreaded Enemies

The scale needle has started down again—not quite a pound—but, praise the Lord, it is descending. How upsetting to record a higher weight today than a week ago! However, I found a verse that shows me I'm not alone when it comes to backsliding:

> But now that you know God ... how is it that you are turning back to those weak and miserable principles? Do you wish to be enslaved by them all over again? (Gal. 4:9).

Paul was referring to the Galatians who were returning to the law for their righteousness and salvation rather than trusting Christ, but this verse drew my attention because of my behavior while we had company. I turned back to the former way! I was almost as gluttonous as I was before I heard of the food program. I turned back to the old way of eating. Why? Because I associated former happy times and these relatives with overeating. I didn't ask God for advice, so I failed to see the coming of visitors as an opportunity for the Devil to take over.

When I quit drinking and smoking I came to a place where I realized alcohol and nicotine were my dreaded enemies. Only then could I get victory. I know I am weak and it's possible for me to go back to these habits, so I still pray for protection from becoming a slave to either.

In the same way, I now must come to the place where I am totally convinced that sugar, chocolate, and fat are also dreaded enemies.

Jesus! Help me never to turn back again. Unmask Satan so I can recognize my dreaded enemies and never be enslaved by them again.

Loving Me

Joe and I did some clean-up work at church Sunday afternoon. It took us longer than we expected, and, just as we were finishing, Gary, one of the high-school boys, drove up for evening church.

"We'd better get home before someone else sees us in these dirty clothes," Joe said. I began to put our tools in the car.

"Aren't you staying for church?" Gary asked.

"In our grubbies?" I answered.

"Aw. You'll miss our program."

"Are you in it?" Joe asked.

"Givin' my testimony."

Joe and I looked at each other. "We could buy clothes across the street," I said. We did! During church we were so blessed by their testimonies we hated for the service to end. (And I was really blessed when I saw what size I now wear!)

Love your neighbor as yourself.... Live by the Spirit, and you will not gratify the desires of the sinful nature (Gal. 5:14, 16).

Do I love myself? I was brought up to have a false humility—never brag on self, always be demure and self-effacing. But the verse says to love my neighbor—to love Gary and the high-school boys—as myself. God must want me to love myself. And why not? He made me. In the doctor's office I was looking at charts of the human skeleton and nervous system. I was overwhelmed by the body's intricate design. How could God make even one body, much less millions and millions and millions? When I consider how marvelous the body is, my body, I see it as a treasure. God gave me this treasure to protect and nourish and use. Why would I ever want to abuse it? Of course, I don't consciously abuse it, but too often I simply forget to love myself.

Holy Spirit, I do want to live as You direct. I sincerely invite You to live in my marvelous body today, so I will not gratify my sinful nature.

Look-Alike

When I awoke this morning I had a sore throat and stuffy nose. First cold of the season. I remembered the old saying "Feed a cold," and thought it was an excellent excuse to enjoy a big bowl of hot oatmeal with sugar and cream. When I took my temperature, however, I recalled the rest of the motto—"and starve a fever."

So I had my usual breakfast—bran cereal with non-fat milk, fruit, and one slice of whole grain toast. Satisfying and delicious. It's been several months now since I started on this program, and I am stabilizing. I feel settled, have fewer bad times, and, aside from this pesky cold, I feel good. I praise God for this. Best of all, I know I am growing spiritually.

So God created man in his own image, in the image of God he created him; male and female he created them (Gen. 1:27).

Some say God has a body like ours (or visa versa), and others say this Scripture refers to our spirits or personalities. Either way, how wonderful to know I was designed like God. Friends tell me I look more like my mother everyday—I wonder if I am becoming more like God everyday? I don't know if I look like God, but I'm certain of one thing: When He created me, He didn't throw in any fat—I've done that to myself.

O perfect Father! I give You my praise. I want to look like You and be like You—yet the thought is beyond my understanding. Help me today to grow more like You. Help me not to use this cold as an excuse to overeat.

Handwork

When I told Joan I had a cold, she said, "I always get a cold when I diet." After we hung up, I thought about that and decided maybe I did need to eat a little more. *Ah, deceitful heart.* Without allowing myself to think it through, much less ask the Lord, I made and ate two pieces of toast. They tasted good; going down, they eased my sore throat, but I regret it, because it means either no meat for dinner tonight or no vegetables and fruit. Either way, I have hurt myself—and to think, yesterday I said I was stabilizing!

He who has been stealing must steal no longer, but must work, doing something useful with his own hands, that he may have something to share with those in need (Eph. 4:28).

At first reading, I didn't see that this verse applied to me—then I felt as if I had been slapped. The Holy Spirit was telling me I am a thief! I am supposed to have only three meals a day, but how often I open the refrigerator, stare at the food, then break off a piece of bread or eat a spoonful of cottage cheese or munch a handful of grapes. How often I go to the cupboard, stare at the shelves, then have some crackers, Fritos, or a few peanuts. That doesn't seem so bad, but, more often than not, *I don't count those calories.* I am a thief, stealing my own calorie ration. How deceitful—and how stupid. The Bible says I must steal no more. But I get so hungry between meals. When I am tempted to take "bites" of food, I am either going to have to count the calories or do something to take my mind off food. The Bible verse says to do something useful with my hands.

Instead of opening the refrigerator door, I *could* wash it! Instead of opening the cupboard doors I could wipe them down. Better still, I could get out of the kitchen. I could dust the blinds, or clean the bathroom or go outside and water—anything to make my home a nicer place for my husband. The key to stealing no more is *labor.*

Lord, lately You've shown me, almost every day, how deceitful I am. Help me to be true to myself and true to You.

Wising Up

When Joe came home last night he said, "What's different? Have you changed the furniture around?"

"No. Why?"

"Something is different. It's roomier."

I laughed with pleasure, and also embarrassment. All I'd done was take the magazines off the end tables, put the books back up on their shelves, vacuum, and dust! The living room did look bigger, and better. Best of all, while I was straightening it up, I was doing something with my hands besides opening cupboard doors.

Be very careful, then, how you live—not as unwise but as wise, making the most of every opportunity, because the days are evil. Therefore do not be foolish, but understand what the Lord's will is (Eph. 5:15–17).

How do the unwise live? For one thing they live as if there were no tomorrow. They don't take care of their bodies. Some drink alcohol and burn up their brains; some smoke and fill their lungs with tar; some use drugs and lose their minds. Others simply gorge and get fat (Who, me?) Am I living unwisely? Maybe not as much as I used to, but the danger is always there, because I *have* to eat. An alcoholic, smoker, or drug addict, with God's help, can quit. But I can't swear off food, and it's hard to be wise, to learn to eat the right foods in the right amounts. But God wants me to be wise. He wants me to make the most of every opportunity. With His help, I will. Yesterday I learned the value of keeping busy—doing something with my hands. Here are more things I can do:

Instead of thinking about food, plan ways to witness to certain people. Look up Scriptures and be ready.

Instead of reading recipes in magazines, read Christian literature, such as *Moody Monthly, Guideposts, Virtue.*

Instead of watching TV, knit, paint, sew, write a letter, or take a walk. (Most urges to eat in the evening come from commercials.)

Instead of eating a snack, pray, exercise, get out the church roll and call someone who has been absent, pay bills, or reconcile the checkbook.

> Only one life—'twill soon be past
> Only what's done for Christ will last.
> (Unknown)

Lord Jesus, I want to be careful, wise, and understand what Your will is. (In my natural state I am careless, unwise, and in the dark.) Help me this day to attain these goals.

Sow and Reap

As I looked at my body in the mirror, gratitude warmed me. The saddles on my hips were smaller, and the roll around my waist was gone! "Thank You, Lord!" I whispered. Then Satan whispered back, "How long can you keep it off? A month? Six months? Be sure, it will come back." Fear erased my smile. How long will I be able to keep it off? When will I "fall off the wagon" and start gaining? But wait a minute. Didn't I learn months ago that Jesus had begun a good work in me? If it was really God who started this plan, He will carry it on to completion—until I go home to be with Him or He comes for me in the Rapture. No more fat days for me—if I step back and let Jesus get on with His work. Stepping back involves not pushing myself forward. Stepping back is saying, "You go first, Jesus. Wherever You go is all right with me."

Since they would not accept my advice and spurned my rebuke, they will eat the fruit of their ways and be filled with the fruit of their schemes (Prov. 1:30–31).

I don't want to ignore God's advice ever again. Since His nature is long-suffering and loving, I have often disobeyed Him about food, whining like a spoiled child, "Lord, I know this is fattening, but, *somehow*, keep it from making me gain." Did He keep me from gaining when I ate fattening foods? No. God has laws of nature which are irrefutable. If I drop a pencil, it will fall to the floor. If I overeat, I will get overweight.

O God, help me to listen and accept Your advice; help me to learn that I will reap what I sow.

SUCH AN INNOCENT
LOOKING BOTTLE...
BUT YOU SAY
A TWELVE OUNCE
SOFT DRINK HAS
EIGHT TEASPOONS
OF SUGAR?...
I'LL TRADE YOU
FOR SOME ICE
WATER.

Fear Not!

Sister-in-law Pat shared with me what she has learned about fear. "The phrase *fear not* is in the Bible over fifty times," she said. "And it's always a command from the Lord. He didn't say, 'I'd rather you not fear,' but, 'Fear not.' So when we say we're afraid of this or that, we're disobeying His command."

Shock! I began to listen to my use of "fearful" words.

"I'm afraid it's going to be hot today.

"I'm worried we won't be able to pay all the bills.

"I'm afraid I'm going to get David's cold."

Besides that, I live with one constant fear: I'm afraid I'm going to gain weight. What trust. What faith! Thanks, Pat, for bringing this to my attention. I'm not only going to have to watch my weight, but watch my mouth.

So do not fear, for I am with you; do not be dismayed, for I am your God. I will strengthen you and help you; I will uphold you with my righteous right hand (Isa. 41:10).

He not only tells me to fear not, He promised to strengthen and help me, to uphold me with His righteous right hand! Would God lie? If I tell Him how afraid I am of gaining weight and ask Him to strengthen my determination to lose, would He let me fail? Not my God! He is upholding me (I see Him holding me up, restraining me from opening the refrigerator) with His own righteous hand. I wonder why the Holy Spirit added "righteous." Wasn't *right hand* a strong enough term? Maybe He wanted to underscore the contrast between the evil of my self-effort and the great goodness of my allowing God to do it.

Dear God, with Your help I will not fear. I will not be dismayed. I know You are my God and will strengthen and hold me with Your righteous right hand.

Sticks to Snakes

Since I've been "watching my mouth," I've caught myself using "fearful" language. "I'm afraid we're due for a big earthquake." Or, "I doubt the inflation will ever get better." All these years I thought I was a cheerful person! "Fear not" has certainly put a spotlight on my true self.

Yet deep inside, I do have an abiding peace, an optimism that everything is okay. Maybe I'm influenced to speak negatively so I can be in line with others around me. I really don't want my neighbors to think I'm a little bit crazy. And that's what they would think if I told them that I believe *all* things work for good, that I am not afraid to die, that I am looking forward to seeing Jesus and inspecting my mansion in the sky. The Scripture makes me think, and I am beginning to know and believe what I *say* I believe!

Never will I leave you; never will I forsake you (Heb. 13:5).

As I was with Moses, so I will be with you; I will never leave you or forsake you (Josh. 1:5).

How ridiculous some of my praying is. So often I pray, "O Lord, just be with me." Am I calling Him a liar? In many verses He has already promised His presence. So why do I ask Him to be with me? Don't I really believe He is here at all times? Is He with me just during devotions, or does He stay with me while I prepare meals, make beds, do laundry? Is He with me even when I binge? Or does He leave me to suffer alone? "As I was with Moses, so I will be with you," the Lord promised. How was He with Moses? He empowered Moses to: change sticks to snakes, rivers to blood, and the sea to dust—just a few things like that. Why do I behave as though He weren't with me? "As I was with Moses." Moses called to the Lord in every problem. He had such confidence in God that He stood up and told the people (thousands of them), "Do not be afraid. Stand firm and you will see the deliverance the Lord will bring" (Exod. 14:13).

Dear God, as I get nearer to my weight goal, it seems harder to lose an ounce than it was, at first, to lose a pound. But You are here—You know all about it. Help me to stand firm. Let me see your deliverance.

Celebration

At last! Oh, wonderful day. I've reached my goal. Thank You, thank You, Lord! I weigh less than I did when I graduated from high school! I want to celebrate! I deserve to celebrate. Joe would want me to celebrate. We could go to the steak house and have soup, salad, prime rib, baked potatoes with gobs of sour cream and butter, hot rolls, a side order of fried zucchini, and for dessert, Black Forest cake a' la mode! It would be just like old times!

We remember the fish we ate in Egypt . . . also the cucumbers, melons, leeks, onions and garlic. But no . . . we never see anything but this manna! (Num. 11:5–6).

Yes, I want to celebrate. But not by gorging. Not by "going back to Egypt." As I look back and remember the days in which I failed, I know I don't want to repeat them. I remember the binges were always triggered by lustful reminiscing about forbidden foods, and negligence in studying my Bible and praying. Just as I know that I dare not have even a glass of wine lest I fall into a life of alcoholism, I know I can never return to the old eating habits or leave God out of my decisions and expect to stay slender.

Lord God! Thank You for the victory. I pray, as You took Your people out of the Enemy's hand, keep me safe and moving on toward the Promised Land.

Epilogue

As I read over these meditations I was surprised how similar they all are. Yet, when I wrote them, each one seemed fresh and special. They all have the same problem . . . a new day with new temptations. They all have the same solution . . . a Bible verse to warn or encourage and a prayer for help. Repetitious! Why go through it every day? Why can't I just say, "Lord, You know my problem, so watch over me today"? I don't know. But I do know that on the days I don't take time for Scripture, meditation, and prayer, I fail. I also fail if I go through the quiet time mechanically. I have to really get serious with God before I receive His help. I guess that's what James meant when he said, "Effective prayer can accomplish much."

My prayer now is that others, whether ten pounds or a hundred pounds overweight, will be encouraged—first to learn all they can about nutrition, then to start meeting with the Lord every morning to receive His strength to get rid of those extra pounds . . . for His glory.